written by
LEISA STEWART-SHARPE

illustrated by
LUCY ROSE

COMEBACK CREATURES

DISCOVER THE WILD THINGS ONCE THOUGHT EXTINCT

WIDE EYED EDITIONS

> "**EXTINCTION** IS THE RULE. **SURVIVAL** IS THE EXCEPTION."
>
> — CARL SAGAN, PLANETARY SCIENTIST

CONTENTS

6 Nature's Lost and Found

8 Making a Comeback

10 The Quest for Missing Nature

12 A Secret on Sulawesi

14 The Long-Lost Pygmy Tarsiers

16 Rainforest Recluses

18 The Night Shrieker of Nonsuch Island

20 The Cahow Makes a Comeback

22 Island Escapees

24 Forgotten in the Forests of Ecuador

26 Hope for the Horned Marsupial Frog

28 Hopping Back From the Dead

30 The Night Walker of Cuba

32 The Cuban Solenodon That Survived

34 Surprises in the Sea

36 The Legend that Lives in Iran

38 The Caspian Horse Rides Again

40 Wandering the Wild West

42 The Terror of New Caledonia

44 Return of the Terror Skink

46 Rediscovering Reptiles

48 Djibouti's Desert Dweller

50 In Search of Sengis

52 The Lost Fishes

54 Hiding in Congo's Green Abyss

56 Bouvier's Red Colobus Photographed

58 Take Our Word for It

60 Treasure in New Zealand's Tussocks

62 The Takahē Takes a Stand

64 From the Back of Beyond

66 Lost in the Land of Dragons on Fernandina Island

68 Finding Fernanda

70 This is Not the End

72 Meanwhile, in a Laboratory . . .

74 You Can Be a Wildlife Detective!

76 Glossary

NATURE'S LOST AND FOUND

Earth is a world of land and sea, of light and dark, of life and death. For the many millions of species flying, flowering, swimming, stomping, climbing, clawing, growling, or growing on Earth in this very moment . . . some scientists estimate that possibly thousands are vanishing each year. They're gone, presumed extinct, lost for good. It's the way of the living world – after all, more than 90 per cent of all organisms that have ever lived on this planet are not alive today. Yet humans have sped up the extinction process, as, among other things, pollution, habitat destruction and climate change caused by modern life, collide with the wild. And once a species is declared extinct, it's gone for good. Or is it?

Years can pass, often centuries, and in some cases millions of years, and a wild thing won't be spotted – not even once. It's assumed extinct. Then, quite unexpectedly, in some unmapped or untrodden corner of the world . . .

. . . the wild thing comes back.

On a treacherous island, a giant tortoise trudges across a lava field. She's the very last of her kind.

In an African desert, a mouse with a trunk scarpers across a rockface, lured back from extinction with a scoop of peanut butter.

And on a mountain slope, scientists spy a beast they thought was lost forever: a deer . . .
with fangs.

Tiny horses, singing dogs, giant earthworms, and many more creatures all making the most extraordinary comebacks. And now is your chance to find them.

Venture to untamed corners of the planet, following in the footsteps of science, and come face to face with ten fantastical creatures that, against all odds, have made the most astounding comebacks. First, travel to their wild homes and explore the surrounding habitats, before turning the page to discover the creature's secret hideout. Throughout the book, special pages will introduce even more unusual Comeback Creatures determinedly clinging on.

This book is a testament to their most unexpected survival.

MAKING A COMEBACK

The remarkable creatures in this book each have their own unique comeback stories, but thanks to their survival, they all belong to a rather exclusive group: the Lazarus taxa.

This name stems from the Bible story about a man named Lazarus, who died from illness and was laid to rest inside a cave that was then sealed shut with a heavy stone. Upset by Lazarus' death, Jesus, the son of God, came to visit him four days later, and that's when it's said a miracle occurred . . . Lazarus rose from the dead. He stepped out of the cave and into the light.

Drawing from that story, palaeontologists began to call a plant or animal that miraculously reappears after being believed extinct a 'Lazarus taxon'. Perhaps the most famous is an enormous fish called a coelacanth (pronounced see-luh-kanth). Everyone thought it had been wiped out with the dinosaurs over 65 million years ago, until one was caught in a fishing net in South Africa in 1938.

coelacanth

Bouvier's red colobus monkey

Scientists like to organize living things into groups that share certain characteristics. They call a group a 'taxon' or 'taxa' (plural).

Scientists went into a tailspin – a prehistoric fish had been found alive and virtually unchanged from its fossil form, as though it had risen from the dead!

And the coelacanth is not alone, as many previously extinct species are rediscovered in this way. Lazarus taxa that somehow survived.

Maybe these clever wild things, though presumed extinct, figured out how to survive somewhere else. Then, *surprise*! They reappeared where humans least expected them. Or *maybe* there were so few of them in the first place they became impossible to find; they were hiding out of sight.

horned marsupial frog

sengi

THE QUEST FOR MISSING NATURE

When a plant or animal species is no longer showing up as a fossil in the layers of Earth's rocks, it's said to have 'disappeared from the fossil record', and scientists begin to think it might have gone extinct. But fossils are a snapshot of the past, and on their own are not enough for scientists to declare a species extinct. *They need more evidence.* So, like wildlife detectives, they set off in search of missing nature.

WATCHING AND WAITING

Scientists search for clues, following footprints, studying scat and peering into nests and burrows in search of life. Sometimes they use special tools, from camera traps and live traps, to drones, satellite images, and even checking for DNA in the soil. They also consider if habitat loss might have unfortunately led to species loss, too. It often involves a lot of watching and waiting.

EUREKA!

Sometimes a simple sighting becomes a phenomenal rediscovery! Then there's no time to lose to ensure the species is not lost again. It begins with counting: how many creatures are there in total, and how many are breeding adults? Do the experts need to step in and help boost species numbers through breeding programmes? And should the habitat be protected as a national park, or can the local communities help as nature guardians?

STOCKY SURVIVOR

In 1997, scientists ventured into India's forests following a hunch. They'd realized previous habitat searches for India's endemic forest owlet were incomplete, as not all its known habitats had been checked before it was declared extinct. After ten days of searching, and over a century since it was last seen, the scientists looked up to find a small, stocky owl perched at the top of a bare tree. The forest owlet had survived.

FINDING HOPE

Some experts predict we are losing between 200 and 2,000 species every year – and those are just the ones we know about. With more than 46,300 species threatened with extinction at the time of writing, the rediscovery of Lazarus taxa gives us much-needed hope that, with enough time and space, even the most endangered creatures could stage staggering comebacks.

All is not lost – long live the Comeback Creatures! Now, let's go and find them.

A SECRET ON SULAWESI

From above, the hard-to-reach Indonesian island of Sulawesi (pronounced soo-la-weh-see) seems to sprawl like a starfish, its four, arm-like peninsulas jutting into the deep Pacific Ocean. It's a place of sugarcane-lined swamps, of rivers that snake through deep gorges, and of mossy mountain forests. Habitats hiding wild things found nowhere else on the planet . . .

Because of its isolation, a staggering 62 per cent of Sulawesi's mammals and 33 per cent of its birds have evolved to be endemic (found only in this place).

A barrel-shaped babirusa snuffles through the swamp forest looking for fruit. Its name means 'pig deer', which explains the long legs and terrifying tusks. All four of the male babirusa's upper canine teeth can grow long enough to curl back and pierce its own skull.

In the forest, a lined gliding lizard scampers up a tree. Unfurling wing-like skin folds, it leaps and soars!

In the lowland rainforest, a *rainbow* seems to appear in the hollow of a tree. It's the rare and rowdy Sulawesi wrinkled hornbill. The colourful 'helmet' at the top of its bill, called a casque, creates an echo chamber that carries its loud call across the forest.

Joining the jungle chorus in the northeastern tip of the island are the critically endangered crested black macaques. They communicate noisily with chuckles, grunts and barks.

Although each of these wild things is reclusive and rare, Sulawesi hides an even more secretive creature. Like a ghost, this gremlin-like animal silently moves through the misty mountains under the cover of night. But over time sightings dwindled, with the last spotted alive in around 1921. Fearing it had vanished from the wild for good, in 2008 scientists set off on an expedition to be sure. They strung-up hundreds of fine, almost invisible 'mist nets' throughout Sulawesi's cloud forests. These mesh nets are normally used to safely capture, then study birds. But this time, they caught something else . . .

THE LONG-LOST PYGMY TARSIERS

Six enormous amber eyes stared down at the scientists, like full moons shining through the mist. They had found not one but three long lost pygmy tarsiers – the gremlin-like creatures they were searching for! A Comeback Creature had been found. No bigger than a tennis ball, these furballs are among the smallest and rarest of the world's tarsier species.

The tarsiers were carefully fitted with radio collars so that the scientists could track them through the moss-covered forests, and discover . . .

Instead of nails, pygmy tarsiers have claws at the ends of their spindly fingers to better grip slippery tree trunks.

As nocturnal animals, pygmy tarsiers have evolved to have big eyes to see in the dark, but their eyeballs are too big to rotate. Instead, they turn their heads 180 degrees in both directions.

When woken from a nap, pygmy tarsiers furl and unfurl their ears as though stretching.

Pygmy tarsiers are now off the extinction list, though not out of danger, as around 80 per cent of Sulawesi's forests have been destroyed or damaged by farming, logging and mining. Scientists and conservationists are fighting to protect the rainforest for the tarsiers, and any other Comeback Creatures still hiding out of sight.

RAINFOREST RECLUSES

ENDANGERED FOREST DWELLERS

Technology has helped us to see far flung corners of our planet, yet patches still remain unexplored. And the harder they are to reach, the more likely they are to hide a Lazarus species.

Rainforests make especially good hideouts. We already know that at least half of the world's wildlife call rainforests home – perhaps 30 million species. But what *don't* we know? What lost species are hiding beneath the thick canopy, behind a cascading waterfall or at the bottom of a slippery gorge? And if we find them, should these species stay secret for their own protection?

1. One night in 2005, while hiking through pristine cloud forest in the Andes Mountains in Ecuador, scientists spied a **Pinocchio lizard** crossing the road – a species not seen for around fifty years. It's so named because the males have a long proboscis (nose) resembling the famous puppet. Sadly, its unusual appearance has made it a target for the pet trade, fetching a high price for smugglers. Now scientists and conservationists must educate people that the lizard is worth so much more to the world when left free in the forest.

2. In 2019, in an ancient cloud forest in Rwanda, central Africa, scientists rediscovered the odd-looking and critically endangered **Hill's horseshoe bat**, not seen for forty years. Like the Pinocchio lizard, this bat has an unusual nose. The horseshoe-shaped flap, called a 'nose leaf', works like a funnel to help the bat focus its echolocation calls to navigate and find food. By recording the bat's call, the scientists can use it to help detect and protect other Hill's horseshoe bats flying through the forest.

3. In 2016, scientists ventured into the vanishing rainforests of the Malawi Hills in East Africa to find the long-lost **Chapman's pygmy chameleon**, not seen since its discovery twenty-four years earlier. Measuring barely the length of a golf tee, scientists discovered not one or two, but seventeen pygmy chameleons tucked in the leaf litter on the forest floor! The species is now on the critically endangered list as scientists fight to save its forest home from farming.

THE NIGHT SHRIEKER OF NONSUCH ISLAND

Lazily stretching through the crystal-clear waters of the north Atlantic Ocean is the Bermuda archipelago – a chain of 181 islands and islets, including windswept Nonsuch Island. As well as being an oasis for nature, in the 1600s it became a sanctuary for shipwrecked humans. The castaways hungrily devoured the island's seabirds and turtles. Later, once the island was permanently settled, introduced species such as rats then ate the turtle and bird eggs. As the years passed, forests were cleared and the island's wild things were pushed to the edge of extinction. Then, in 1963, conservationists saw an opportunity to do something quite radical . . . to make the island wild again!

Nonsuch Island was one of the world's first rewilding projects, as introduced species were removed, native vegetation was replanted, and species once lost were reintroduced.

On the forest floor, a tiny lesser Bermuda land snail inches through the leaf litter. Believed to have gone extinct in the wild in the early 2000s, a breeding programme saw it returned to its forest home in 2020.

The island's 'crab cruncher' silently stalks its prey. It's a yellow-crowned night heron, reintroduced to keep the island's growing red land crab population under control. It grabs a crab, shakes off its shell and swallows it whole.

In the 1960s, thirty years after green sea turtles went extinct in Bermuda, conservationists relocated tens of thousands of green sea turtle eggs from Costa Rica to Nonsuch Island. It was hoped the hatched turtles would return to the island to nest. But as the years passed, no nests were found. Then, in 2015, nearly one hundred green sea turtles unexpectedly hatched on a nearby beach. Could nesting turtles be starting to return? Time will tell.

But for many years something was still missing. A creature with a high-pitched screech so eerie, sailors who heard it believed evil spirits haunted Bermuda's islands. Yet, after centuries of being hunted, the shrieks went silent. For 300 years the creature was believed extinct, until 1951, when a museum team launched an expedition after hearing reports of sightings.
They braved gale-force winds and churning seas to reach the island. On scaling its rocky cliffs, they spied a footprint leading into a tunnel. And as they peered inside, they came face to face with the long-lost creature . . .

THE CAHOW MAKES A COMEBACK

A small, unassuming grey bird was sitting on an egg – a cahow (pronounced kuh-hau), the very animal the scientists were searching for. Another Comeback Creature had been discovered, and it was not the only one!

But even though the cahow was back from the dead, it was not out of danger. Rats had returned to the island, eating the cahow's eggs. And even after they were eliminated, something was still killing the chicks. Another seabird was to blame: white-tailed tropicbirds were nesting inside the cahows' rocky burrows, injuring their young. And so, scientists fitted small wooden doorways to the burrows, just big enough for a cahow to squeeze through. The scientists soon learned . . .

When cahow chicks finally fledge, they skim across the waves feeding on small squid and fish, not returning to the islands for up to five years.

Cahows are rarely seen, as they leave and return to their islands under the cover of night.

There are now over 150 breeding pairs of cahows on Bermuda's islands, with over seventy chicks fledging annually – a conservation triumph, given females lay only one egg a year. And the night skies are once again filled with the cahow's startling cries.

ISLAND ESCAPEES

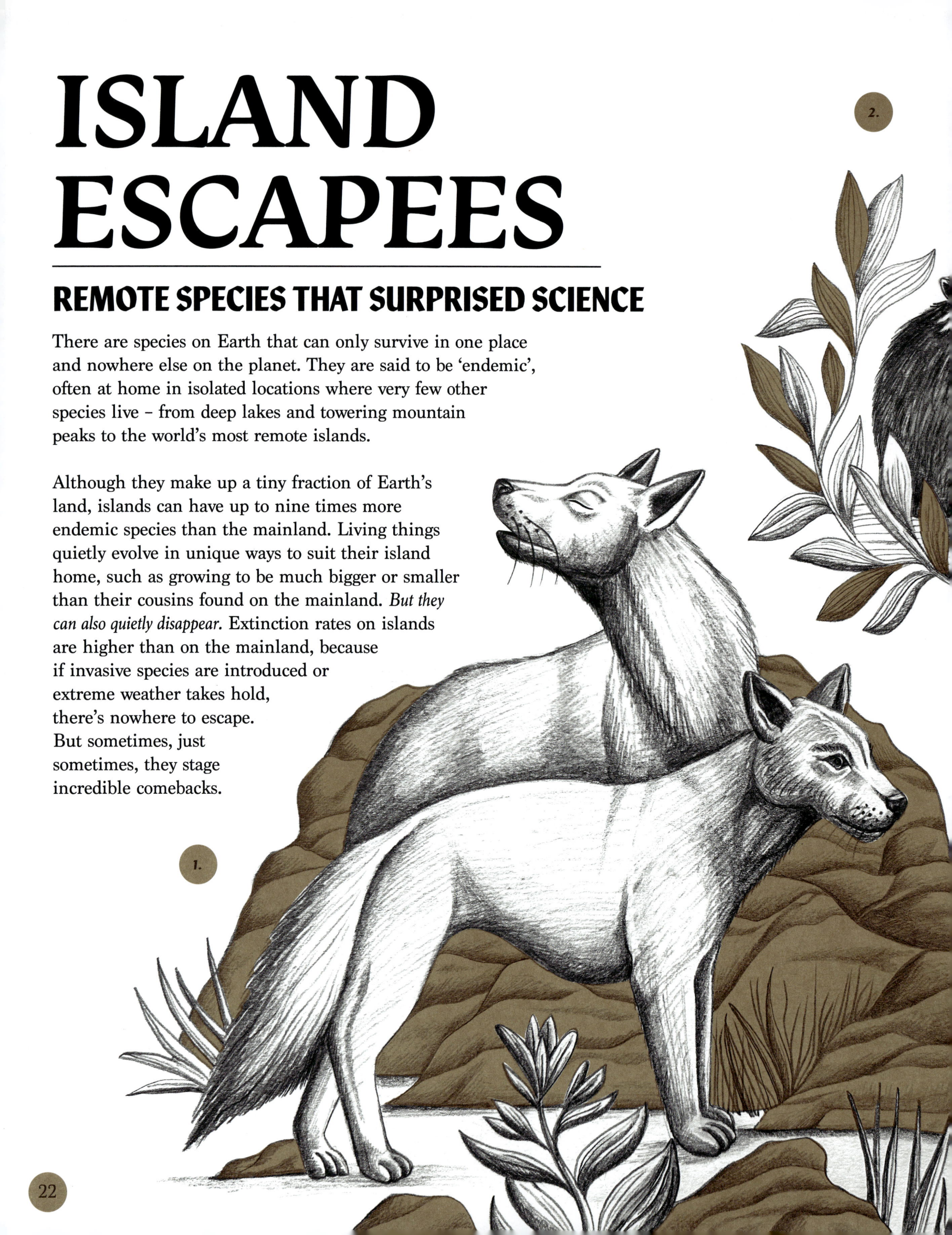

REMOTE SPECIES THAT SURPRISED SCIENCE

There are species on Earth that can only survive in one place and nowhere else on the planet. They are said to be 'endemic', often at home in isolated locations where very few other species live – from deep lakes and towering mountain peaks to the world's most remote islands.

Although they make up a tiny fraction of Earth's land, islands can have up to nine times more endemic species than the mainland. Living things quietly evolve in unique ways to suit their island home, such as growing to be much bigger or smaller than their cousins found on the mainland. *But they can also quietly disappear.* Extinction rates on islands are higher than on the mainland, because if invasive species are introduced or extreme weather takes hold, there's nowhere to escape. But sometimes, just sometimes, they stage incredible comebacks.

1. Eerie cries carry over the mountains of New Guinea in the Pacific Ocean. They belong to the **New Guinea singing dog**, believed to have gone extinct in the wild in the 1970s because its forest home had been cleared. Then, in 2012, a tour guide stumbled across a lone dog roaming the slopes over 4,200 metres above sea level. Four years later, scientists discovered a pack of these wild dogs on their trail cameras and, after fitting radio collars, now track their movements for their protection.

2. The rare, long-limbed monkey known as **Miller's grizzled langur** was presumed extinct in 2005 after scientific search parties failed to find it on the Indonesian island of Borneo in the Java Sea. Then, in 2011, scientists were shocked to see the white, bristly beard of these langurs on camera trap footage taken in an area well outside their known range. The world's rarest primate was back from extinction!

3. A tiny glass-like flower called a **fairy lantern** shines on the forest floor, on the island country of Japan off the east coast of continental Asia. With no leaves to turn the Sun's rays into energy, it instead steals the nutrients it needs to grow by tapping into the underground fungi network. It was assumed extinct after an industrial estate was built on its habitat, only for a student to spy one thirty years later on a nearby forest trail.

FORGOTTEN IN THE FORESTS OF ECUADOR

There is a place that time forgot in the foggy forests of Ecuador in Central America. Here, habitats dramatically vary with the steep slopes of the Andes Mountains, creating some of the greatest biodiversity levels on the planet. From a volcano's snow-capped summit and misty cloud forests, down to steamy tropical jungles and wet lowland forests, this is the protected Cotacachi Cayapas (pronounced koh-tah-ca-shi kaye-a-pahs) Ecological Reserve.

The Cotacachi Cayapas Nature Reserve covers an area bigger than Greater London, UK, hiding thousands of species.

High up in the misty mountains, cloud forests grow. They are like hanging gardens, as epiphyte (pronounced eh-puh-fite) plants of bromeliads, ferns and orchids dangle from tree branches and trunks, their roots drawing moisture from the damp air all around. Rattles ring out as colourful toucans call to each other through the fog.

Further down the slopes is the trapeze artist of the treetops – a brown-headed spider monkey, dangling by its tail. It then 'walks' along a branch *upside down*. This endangered monkey is also a gardener. It eats fruit, then drops the seeds as it travels through the forest, so that in time new trees can grow.

On the dark forest floor, a giant anteater is clawing open a termite mound. With no teeth, it uses its sticky tongue to lick up the insects inside. It doesn't hear the predator silently moving through the shadows. Closer, and closer, until a sudden whiff of wild cat alerts the anteater, who escapes into the night.

It was just outside the nature reserve, in an untouched patch of Ecuador's Chocó rainforest, that in 2018 scientists heard a *strange* sound. *Bop!* It sounded like a cork popping from a bottle; an animal call unlike any they had ever heard before. *Bop!* The scientists trekked through the thick undergrowth following the sound. *Bop!* They turned their torchlight to the trees, scouring the palm leaves, when finally, the light settled on two shining golden eyes . . .

HOPE FOR THE HORNED MARSUPIAL FROG

The scientists had stumbled upon a grumpy-looking horned marsupial frog (so-called because the horn-like skin flaps above its eyes make the frog appear to frown). This unusual, nocturnal frog was officially declared extinct in 2005, so its discovery that night in 2018 caused the scientists to leap about with excitement. Even more so when they found another three of these frogs, including a pregnant female. The scientists soon learned that . . .

In the same way Australian marsupials (such as kangaroos, wombats and possums) keep their young safe in skin folds called a pouch, female horned marsupial frogs have a 'backpack' pouch.

These frogs live on leaves high up in the canopy, where the humid air prevents their skin from drying out.

A female will carry eggs in her pouch for up to eighty days, allowing her offspring to skip the tadpole phase and emerge into the world as fully formed froglets.

But animals don't understand boundaries, and these frogs were found clinging on in a tiny island of healthy, 'old growth' forest outside the protection of the reserve. Alarmingly, some 98 per cent of the surrounding forest had previously been cut down by humans, and the frogs were now in the danger zone. Fortunately, conservationists are buying sections of the forest to knit together a safe habitat for the frogs forever more.

HOPPING BACK FROM THE DEAD

AMPHIBIANS MAKING A COMEBACK

It's not easy being an amphibian. Since 1970, around 200 species have gone extinct, many because of a frightening fungus called chytrid (pronounced kit-rid) which makes it difficult for frogs and toads to breathe.

But *do not* underestimate our sticky-footed friends. After all, many of their ancestors survived the very asteroid that killed the dinosaurs, and evolved to have freakish superpowers. Some see-through glass frogs can turn invisible by hiding their blood, while wood frogs living in the Arctic freeze to survive the winter. In spring, their bodies thaw and the frogs come back to life! But even more miraculously, with the help of science, some amphibians are hopping back from extinction.

1. In 1996, the black-bellied, white-spotted **Hula painted frog** was declared the first frog species to go extinct. Then in 2011, it leapt out of a lake in Israel in the Middle East and back on to the critically endangered list.

2. Like all midwife toads, the male **Majorcan midwife toad**, on the Spanish island of Majorca, carries the eggs of his unhatched young on a string which he wraps around his back legs. When the eggs are ready to hatch, he drops them off in a pond. This toad was rediscovered in a remote gorge on Majorca in 1979. Before then, scientists only knew of it from a prehistoric fossil.

3. Known as the clown frog, or Halloween frog for its orange and black splodges, the variable **Harlequin toad** was thought to have gone extinct from the deadly chytrid fungus. It was thankfully rediscovered in a mountainous reserve in Costa Rica in Central America in 2004.

4. In 2013, in the aptly named Lazarus Project, Australian scientists attempted to resurrect an extinct frog species not seen alive since 1984. Scientists took DNA from frozen frog tissue and used the eggs from a distantly related frog to bring the **gastric brooding frog** back from extinction for a few days. Unusually, the frog swallows her own eggs. Around twenty-five tadpoles then hatch in her stomach, as she goes on to vomit out her young.

29

THE NIGHT WALKER OF CUBA

Basking in the warm waters of the northern Caribbean Sea is the crocodile-shaped island of Cuba that is just as wild as it looks. Stretching from the island's northeastern shores, through impassable forests that carpet steep mountain slopes, is the Alejandro de Humboldt National Park. Wild and remote, it's one of the most biologically diverse places on Earth, hiding creatures found nowhere else. But first you must find them, for many of them are very, *very* small.

Sometimes, animals endemic to islands evolve to be small because there's less food available to help them grow.

A tiny snail slides through the forest. It's one of six species of painted snails, known for their colourfully swirled shells – this one splendidly striped.

A tiny Gervais' funnel-eared bat leaves its hot and humid cave to hunt flies and mosquitoes in the forest. Weighing as little as three jellybeans, it looks more like a moth than a bat.

On the leafy forest floor, a frog about the size of a fingernail hunts for a microscopic meal: tiny, eight-legged bugs known as mites that produce a natural toxin. The Monte Iberia dwarf frog eats the mites, then releases their poison through its skin to defend itself against predators such as snakes.

The world's smallest bird flits from flower-to-flower sipping nectar, its iridescent feathers sparkling in the sun. It's a bee hummingbird, no bigger than a walnut. Its wings flutter at an astounding eighty times a second, creating a 'buzz' as it flies upside down, and even *backwards*.

While Cuba is an ideal refuge for the splendidly small, there's a larger creature here that scampers through the night. It's a scientific oddity from the time of the dinosaurs that somehow *survived*. Due to its rarity, the creature was believed extinct until 1974, when one individual inside the national park stumbled back on to science's radar . . .

THE CUBAN SOLENODON THAT SURVIVED

A stocky furball with a long snout zigzagged through the undergrowth on its tiptoes. It was a Cuban solenodon, barely changed from the mammal that scurried beneath the feet of the dinosaurs more than 70 million years ago.

The name solenodon comes from the Greek word for 'grooved tooth', for just like snakes, the solenodon injects venomous saliva through its serrated teeth to injure or kill its prey, including insects, grubs and spiders. Scientists have found just a handful of these rare creatures, revealing . . .

When surprised, solenodons are known to trip head-over-heels.

A solenodon twitters and cheeps like a bird, and is even said to grunt like a pig when under threat.

Although they look like shrews and are closely related to moles, they are a distinct species with their own branch on Earth's evolutionary tree.

Yet the greatest threat to the Cuban solenodon could be that it's largely unknown. With so many of Earth's endangered species desperately needing conservation funding, it's often the more familiar species that get the attention. That's why we need all eyes on unusual Comeback Creatures like this one, to secure their survival.

SUPRISES IN THE SEA

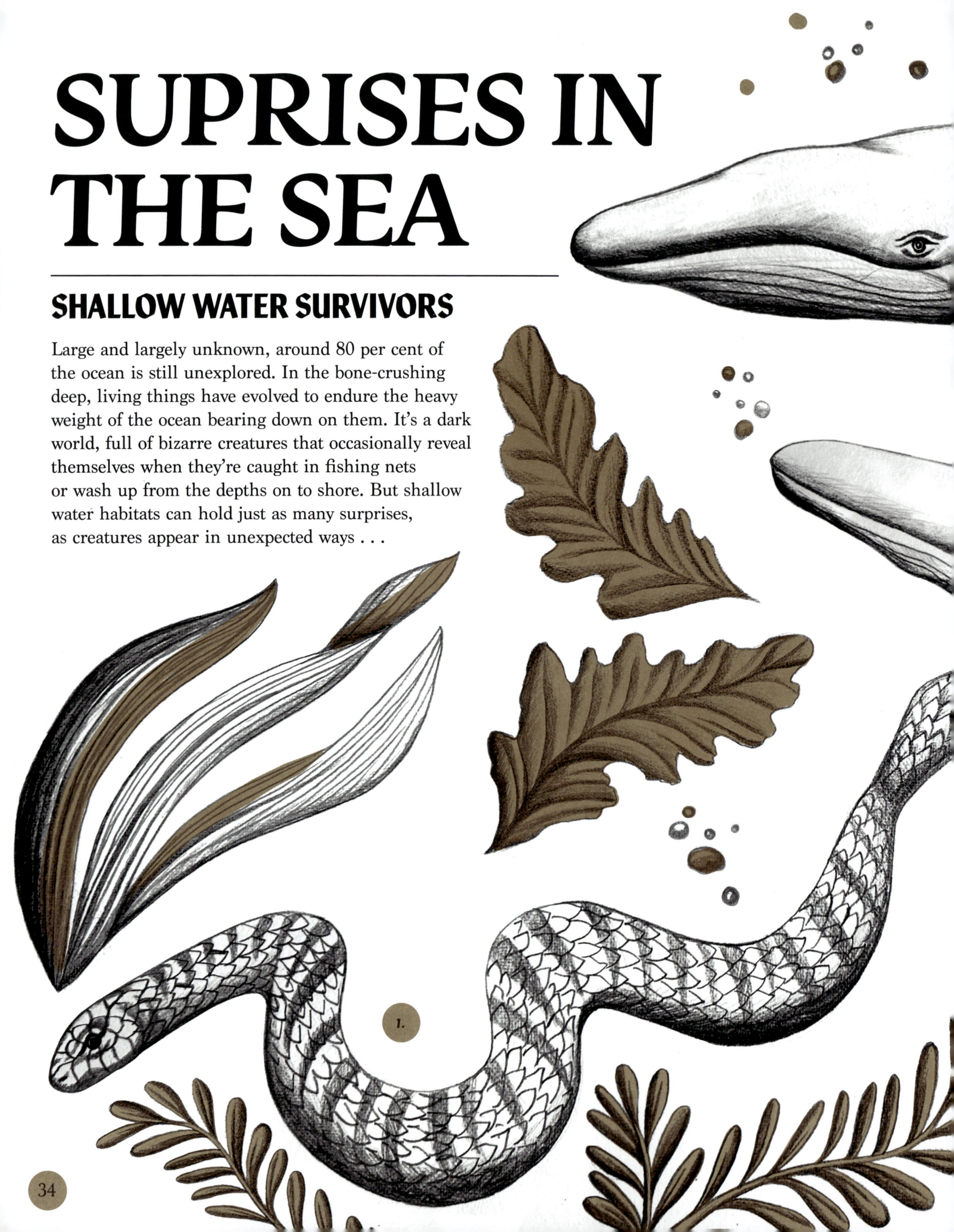

SHALLOW WATER SURVIVORS

Large and largely unknown, around 80 per cent of the ocean is still unexplored. In the bone-crushing deep, living things have evolved to endure the heavy weight of the ocean bearing down on them. It's a dark world, full of bizarre creatures that occasionally reveal themselves when they're caught in fishing nets or wash up from the depths on to shore. But shallow water habitats can hold just as many surprises, as creatures appear in unexpected ways . . .

1.

1. In the Timor Sea, off the western Australian coast, scientists working on a research ship sent a submersible rover some sixty metres down to the seabed. And to their great surprise, the rover sent back images of the **short-nosed sea snake** alive. This sleek swimmer has a very venomous bite, and was believed extinct in the shallow waters of Ashmore Reef for over two decades, possibly because their coral habitat is disappearing. This species was then found surviving in the ocean's Twilight Zone, leading scientists to wonder . . . what other species are seeking refuge in deeper waters?

2. After being initially misidentified as another species in the 1970s, a handful of dead whale specimens were correctly identified in 2003 as a new and unusual species: **Omura's whale**, a small species with a long, slender body. And despite efforts to identify more of them alive, they couldn't be found; scientists feared commercial whaling and fishing had led to their extinction. A decade passed and the legend of the 'ghost whale' grew, until it was eventually assumed extinct. Scientists later realized that whales sighted in the waters off the island of Madagascar in the Indian Ocean in 2011 were in fact Omura's whales!

3. Sponges were some of the first animals to live on Earth, and can usually be found anchored to the seafloor. While some are spongy, many others have hard skeletons resembling delicate glass vases, or in the case of the **Neptune's cup** sponge, a giant goblet. This species once stood over a metre tall and wide in the shallow waters of the Indian and west Pacific Oceans. For years they were brought to the surface and used as babies' bathtubs, until they were assumed extinct in 1907 due to overharvesting. Fortunately, in 2011 divers stumbled across several smaller specimens of the sponges alive, and work to protect them from future extinction has now begun.

THE LEGEND THAT LIVES IN IRAN

In Iran in the Middle East, there's a crescent-shaped mountain range called the Alborz Mountains (meaning 'high watch' in the ancient Persian language). For these mountains stand guard over secrets – rare species living in the high alpine meadows and on lushly forested mountain slopes.

The Alborz Mountains are mountains of two sides: fertile on the rainy northern slopes and dry on the south where they slope down to the desert-like Iranian plateau.

Golden eagles soar over the towering peak of Mount Damāvand. It was once a fiery volcano and is now capped with the last of the winter's snow. In spring its slopes bloom with flowers that dazzle like jewels, and the foothills turn red as a sea of red poppies yawn open in the morning light.

Lower down the Alborz Mountains' northern slopes lies a forest millions of years old. It grows green and tall as it soaks up water from the clouds. When all other forests froze then died during the Ice Ages, this lush Hyrcanian forest survived, sheltered by the Caspian Sea. Today it's one of the planet's oldest forests, from which all others in northern Europe grew.

Deep within the forest, a Persian leopard, the largest of all leopard types, rests on a mossy tree branch. It waits for lunch, a wild goat, to wander by. Patient now . . . wait for it . . . then . . . *pounce!*

And the leopard isn't the only large mammal prowling these mountains. A Syrian brown bear, straw-coloured with distinctive white claws, forages on fruits and berries. This place is one of its last havens as the mountainous forests and grasslands of Asia gradually disappear.

Yet it's where the mountains cradle the shores of the world's largest lake, the Caspian Sea, that a startling discovery was made; a creature from a different time. The animal dated back to the Persian Empire in 3000 BCE, and was believed extinct for thousands of years. After so much time, there was no possible way it could still be alive, could it?

THE CASPIAN HORSE RIDES AGAIN

Dark brown stallions run wild and free along the shores of the Caspian Sea, their silky coats shining in the sun. They are the long-lost Caspian horses. At around a metre tall, these tiny, elegant horses are barely bigger than a pony. The breed was rediscovered in 1965 by a woman searching for small horses for her children's riding school. When she came across this herd, she realized she'd made a monumental discovery. These could be the same breed once used by ancient Persian kings thousands of years ago to pull chariots into battles with lions. As the woman searched the mountains for more of these slender horses, she learnt . . .

Their tough hooves meant they often didn't need to wear horseshoes, making them ideal 'work horses' in the local villages.

The Caspian horse is the ancestral breed for many of today's horses.

Caspian horses were so beloved by their ancient owners that archaeologists have discovered their image in paintings and sculptures.

Today, less than 2,000 of these rare horses exist in the world, and so breeding programmes are underway to help secure their survival.

WANDERING THE WILD WEST

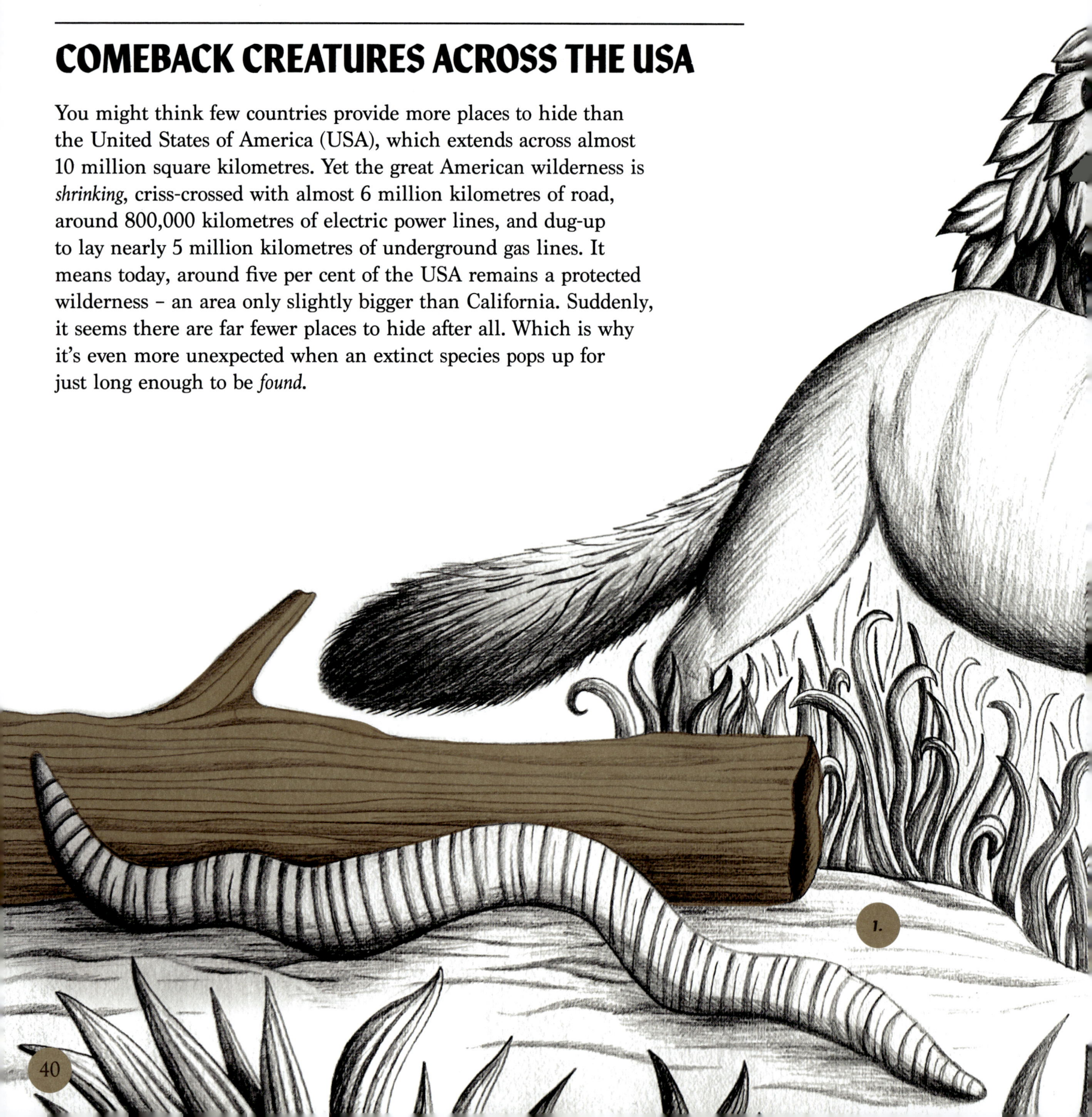

COMEBACK CREATURES ACROSS THE USA

You might think few countries provide more places to hide than the United States of America (USA), which extends across almost 10 million square kilometres. Yet the great American wilderness is *shrinking*, criss-crossed with almost 6 million kilometres of road, around 800,000 kilometres of electric power lines, and dug-up to lay nearly 5 million kilometres of underground gas lines. It means today, around five per cent of the USA remains a protected wilderness – an area only slightly bigger than California. Suddenly, it seems there are far fewer places to hide after all. Which is why it's even more unexpected when an extinct species pops up for just long enough to be *found*.

1. Beneath the prairie grasslands in eastern Washington and north Idaho squirms a ghostly burrower; a see-through worm believed extinct for about two decades, until 2005 when a scientist accidentally put a trowel through one. The 'giant' **Palouse earthworm** was suddenly back from extinction. It was dead, but nonetheless proof that the species had lived. And it was enough for another team of scientists to set out in 2010 to find the worm alive. When they did, they disproved some of the legends that had grown around it; the earthworm doesn't spit, smell like lilies, or stretch to one-metre long. It is, however, under threat, as its prairie habitat is lost to farming and grazing.

2. While scientific expeditions using technology such as camera traps and drones are helping to unearth long-lost animals, extinct creatures have, on occasion, simply turned up in someone's backyard. This was the case in 1981, when a dog in Wyoming left an unusual gift on its owner's back porch – a dead **black-footed ferret**. These ferrets were previously thought to have gone extinct because of the plague, an infectious disease brought to the USA on trading ships in the 1900s. Today, ferrets bred and released in the wild are vaccinated against the plague to give them another shot at survival.

3. A blurry, seconds-long video from 2005, and a few grainy photos since then are the only 'evidence' that the **ivory-billed woodpecker** perhaps didn't go extinct during the 1940s afterall. Several bird experts known as ornithologists have spotted the bird's distinctive white bill and black-and-white feathers in the southern swamps of Louisiana, and have heard its unique 'double knock' as it pecks at the trees. Although authorities maintain the species is extinct, bird-watchers and ornithologists continue to scale trees, send up drones and attempt to snap one clear photograph to prove the woodpecker's concrete comeback.

THE TERROR OF NEW CALEDONIA

There's a speck in the South Pacific Ocean, called the Isle of Pines, among the New Caledonia chain of islands. It's so named for the ancient pine-tree groves that line its shores. On this prehistoric island, a snail- and insect-crunching crocodile once prowled. Although it went extinct some 3,000 years ago, what scientists didn't realize was that another reptile had quietly clawed its way to the top of the food chain. And like a *T. rex* of the ancient forest, it still hides there today.

> The tall Araucaria pines found on the island are like those that existed during the Triassic period when the first dinosaurs roamed.

The ancient forests in this area aren't just limited to land – they stretch beneath the waves. The second largest coral reef on the planet thrives here, a sheer wall of tree-like growths that plunges down into the dim ocean depths. These soft corals, called gorgonians, sway in the current, resembling a forest in a storm.

The knobbly branch of a sea fan appears to have eyes. It's that master of disguise, a pygmy seahorse – perhaps the smallest in the ocean at barely two centimetres long. With its long tail, it clings on as dazzling fish are swept along in the strong current.

In the calmer waters of the lagoon, a 'mermaid' swims through the seagrass. It's an endangered dugong, using its bristly upper lip to uproot seagrass. It eats up to thirty kilograms of seagrass a day, clearing a trail through the meadow as it munches. Occasionally it will stop to stand on its tail, pop its head above the surface and *breathe*.

However, the island's jungled shores revealed an unexpected secret – a terror believed extinct for more than one hundred years. In 2003, scientists launched an expedition to find it. They moved *quietly* through the overgrown forest, clearing paths to avoid twigs that might snap underfoot and alert the creature. Harmless funnel and pitfall traps were set, and the scientists began their search, day and night until . . .

RETURN OF THE TERROR SKINK

. . . the terror skink was finally found! It swaggered through the forest, its silvery scales gleaming in the sun. Stretching almost half a metre long, this super-predator feared nothing and was unquestionably the king of this jungle. The terror skink's scientific name, *Phoboscincus bocourti*, combines the Greek noun 'phobos', meaning fear (possibly because of its unusually large size), with the Latin noun 'scincus', meaning skink, which is a type of lizard.

Its long, curved teeth and tremendous biteforce allows it to pierce the hard shells of land crabs and devour other large lizards.

Despite living on a tiny island, the terror skink isn't easy to find. Perhaps fewer than ten have ever been seen, leading scientists to believe their numbers are limited.

With its island home sitting low in the sea, the terror skink's forest habitat is under threat of being destroyed by cyclones, placing the animal a place on the critically endangered list.

REDISCOVERING REPTILES

SECRET SURVIVORS

Over 300 million years of reptile evolution hangs in the balance as 1,800 of the world's reptile species – a fifth of those currently scurrying and sliding across the planet – face extinction. Habitat loss, hunting, introduced species, and the planet getting hotter through climate change are making it tough for many reptiles to cling on.

But is there more to it? It's thought that reptiles are simply not as beloved by the public for being 'cute'. Money spent on conservation is directed towards more attractive animals. Fortunately, herpetologists are rallying for reptiles – searching high and low to find those that are lost before it's too late.

1. In 2017, the vividly yellow **Jackson's climbing salamander** – nicknamed the 'golden wonder' – was rediscovered in the cloud forests of Guatemala in Central America. It hadn't been glimpsed for forty-two years when a guard at the reserve luckily spotted one while on his lunch break!

2. After ten years on the extinction list, in 2017 a dwarf viper known as the **Albany adder** was rediscovered in a secret strip of grassland in South Africa. The secrecy is to protect the species, as so few of these adders have ever been seen. Their rarity makes them prized as pets among collectors.

3. Also under wraps is the location of the **Victorian grassland earless dragon**, rediscovered in Australia in 2023 after a fifty-year absence. The small, striped lizard lives in abandoned spider burrows, its numbers hard hit by foxes and housing developments popping up on its grassland habitat. Scientists are now using sniffer dogs to locate the lizards for a breeding programme to help save the species.

4. Darkly coloured, shy and only venturing out at night . . . it is **Fugler's shadow snake**, not seen for half a century. Very little was known about it since its discovery in 1969, but in 2019, scientists found it sliding over a moss-covered boulder in the tropical rainforests of Ecuador in South America.

47

DJIBOUTI'S DESERT DWELLER

On the east coast of Africa where the hot winds blow, lies the tiny African nation of Djibouti (pronounced juh-boo-tee). It's an unforgiving landscape, home to volcanoes, and dry desert plains that look more like moonscapes than terrain belonging to this Earth. But as extreme as Djibouti's natural environments are, across the stark, rocky terrain and in the brilliant blue seas, a treasure trove of species await discovery.

While Djibouti's landscapes are hostile for most living things, a rare and rather adorable animal has not only survived . . . but thrived!

The biggest fish found anywhere in the sea cruises over coral reefs in the Gulf of Tadjoura (pronounced ta-joo-rah). It's a whale shark. And while the adults can grow to twenty metres in length, the ones that gather here are tiny – they're juveniles! As the water blooms with plankton, huge numbers of these whale sharks slowly swim through the water with their mouths open wide.

Inland, the cratered, moon-like landscape surrounding Lake Abbe is dotted with steaming limestone 'chimneys'. They formed when magma pushed boiling water through Earth's crust, leaving mineral deposits behind. As inhospitable as this salty lake appears, it's home to an abundance of birds, including hundreds of flamingos that gather in the early morning light.

Over the centuries many lakes dried up, leaving behind cracked clay beds that became the sweeping plains of the Grand Bara Desert. To survive out here, you need to be a true desert specialist, like the gerenuk – a giraffe-like gazelle. Standing on two legs, it stretches its long neck to reach tender leaves high above ground. These and shoots from prickly shrubs will give it almost all the moisture it needs without ever needing to take a drink.

For over half a century, a small and rather unusual mammal went unseen by science, so was declared extinct. Except the scientists were *wrong*. Djibouti's other hardy survivors – its nomadic people who herd livestock – were never in any doubt of the animal's existence; they just needed to be asked. In 2019, the local Djibouti people led scientists across the boulder-filled landscape. They helped set over 1,200 traps baited with peanut butter and oatmeal to catch the creature alive and unharmed. Then, one morning . . .

IN SEARCH OF SENGIS

. . . a sengi was found! Even better, twelve sengis were spotted in a matter of weeks, and the first ever photo of the species was finally taken.

To see one of these creatures is to adore them, for this rodent-sized cutey is more closely related to an elephant than a mouse, earning it the name 'elephant shrew'. It uses its long, trunk-like nose to suck termites, ants and other insects off the ground. Fortunately, because the sengi's natural habitat is inaccessible and inhospitable for humans, they've managed to exist virtually undisturbed. And now, scientists know that . . .

The sengi's spindly hind legs are more suited to a gazelle than a mammal of its tiny size, making it a fast runner.

Sengis are solitary. They live alone amongst the rocks until it's time to find a mate, whom they keep for life.

The sengi possibly uses a tiny tuft of fur on the end of its tail like a little broom to spread its scent and mark its territory.

Although never considered lost to the locals, the sengi was now no longer lost to science, and work could begin on preventing its future extinction.

THE LOST FISHES

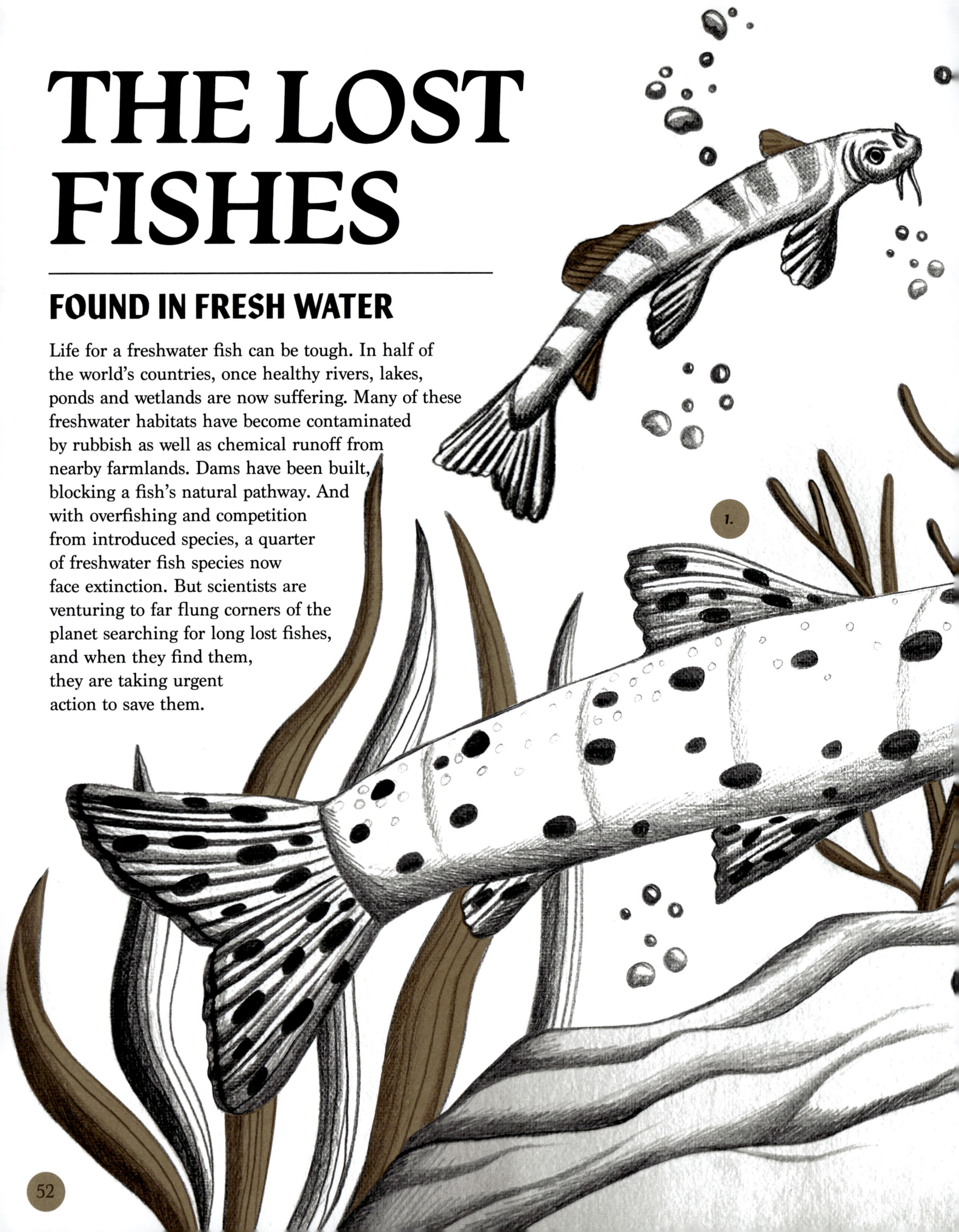

FOUND IN FRESH WATER

Life for a freshwater fish can be tough. In half of the world's countries, once healthy rivers, lakes, ponds and wetlands are now suffering. Many of these freshwater habitats have become contaminated by rubbish as well as chemical runoff from nearby farmlands. Dams have been built, blocking a fish's natural pathway. And with overfishing and competition from introduced species, a quarter of freshwater fish species now face extinction. But scientists are venturing to far flung corners of the planet searching for long lost fishes, and when they find them, they are taking urgent action to save them.

1.

1. For a decade, scientists feared the spotted **leopard barbel** once found in Turkey, in the Middle East, had disappeared for good after nine dams were constructed on its Tigris River home. Then in 2024, a local fisherman caught a fish with black spots and barbel – the tell-tale whiskers that give the fish its name. The leopard barbel had been found.

2. Also in Turkey, the **Batman river loach** – a little fish smaller than a human thumb – had been lost for fifty years. Ichthyologists feared it was gone for good due to river pollution and the construction of a dam. Then, while searching for another fish, a lucky little loach swam into their nets on the first day.

3. In the 1940s, a hydroelectric dam installed on Lake Tazawa in Japan changed acid levels in the water, making it impossible for the **kunimasu salmon** to survive. Sadly, the lake was believed to be the kunimasu's only home. Then, in 2010 scientists were surprised to discover the kunimasu was alive in another lake over 600 kilometres away. Kunimasu eggs had been released into Lake Saiko at the foot of Mount Fuji in 1935. At the time it was believed the fish hadn't survived, but it's now thought thousands thrived.

HIDING IN CONGO'S GREEN ABYSS

Remote and best reached by river are the waterlogged swamp forests of the Congo Basin – Central Africa's Green Abyss. It's so thickly carpeted in tropical plants, it can take twelve hours to trek little more than a kilometre. The going gets even tougher when the wet season arrives, flooding the forest. While inhospitable for most humans, the remote and almost impenetrable swamp forest is ideal for hiding large mammals.

The web of rivers and streams that flow through the Congo Basin flood the forest floor to create the swamp forest.

In 2008, a surprise was found in a secluded corner of the swamp . . . a lost kingdom of gorillas! Tens of thousands of western lowland gorillas were living in the undergrowth of the forest, previously unknown to humans, leading to the creation of a park to protect them.

A bristly hippopotamus waggles its pink ears. It wiles away the heat of the day in the water, where it's protected from sunburn. Yet for an animal that spends most of its life submerged, the hippo cannot swim. It must *walk* through the water, bouncing off the riverbed below.

Hidden in a clearing peppered with puddles is a space known to the indigenous people as a bai. The mineral-rich waters here are like a spa for critically endangered forest elephants that come for a good wallow. The mud cools them down and protects them from insects and the sun.

In 2016, a team of scientists stumbled over submerged roots in waist-deep, leech-infested waters. They were on the trail of a creature believed extinct for over forty years because of hunting. Scratched by spiny palm leaves and stung by coiling liana vines, they persisted, one slow, soggy step at a time. Then, a local tracker appeared with fortunate news: he had spied the creature they were searching for in the forest's deepest reaches. But would they get there in time . . .

BOUVIER'S RED COLOBUS PHOTOGRAPHED

Branches rustled at the top of the canopy, followed by a loud call as a Bouvier's red colobus monkey leapt into view. Fluffy-cheeked and fearless, she stared down at the scientists through a gap in the canopy, with a baby clinging to her belly. Unafraid, she even closed her eyes, just for a moment, before swinging back into the Green Abyss – but not before scientists snapped the first photo of the species.

Scientists not only glimpsed the mother and her infant, but a thriving group.

Of the eighteen species of colobus monkeys, the Bouvier's has distinctive black hands and feet.

Although rediscovered to science, the people of the Congo who fish in its rivers had long known of the monkey's existence.

Fortunately, the monkeys were found inside Ntokou Pikounda, the Congo's newest national park. The local and indigenous communities now keep a watchful eye over their endangered neighbour.

TAKE OUR WORD FOR IT

INDIGENOUS GUARDIANS

Around 476 million indigenous peoples live in over ninety countries around the world, from the Saami of northern Europe and over 300 tribes living in the Amazon rainforest, to the Māori of New Zealand and the Aboriginal and Torres Strait Islanders of Australia.

Generations spent living in nature means indigenous peoples often have a deep understanding of their environment and the wildlife they share it with. This knowledge is proving invaluable, as scientists turn to indigenous groups to help them track down critically endangered species before it's too late. In many cases, they then discover the species was never truly lost – the indigenous peoples always knew where to find them.

1. In the heart of South America are the hot and dry plains of Gran Chaco. Chaco comes from the Quechua (an indigenous language) word *chaku*, which means 'hunting land', as the indigenous tribes hunted many of the animals here for food, including the bristly, pig-like **Chacoan peccary**. Until 1971, scientists only knew of this peccary from fossilized remains, until the indigenous peoples of Argentina led scientists through the thorny scrub to discover the species still alive.

2. In the eastern forest of Afghanistan in the Middle East, a vampire-like creature, believed extinct, somehow survived decades of warfare waged in its natural habitat. It's the small **Kashmir musk deer**, unusual for a deer given the two fangs that hang from its lower jaw. In 2014, scientists asked local people to map where they might find the elusive creature. It led them up a steep rocky outcrop to discover five of the fanged deer hiding in the thicket.

3. In 2015, the Mro, people indigenous to the deeply forested hills of Bangladesh in southern Asia, were given cameras and asked by scientists to photograph any wildlife they would typically meet in a day. They stunned the scientists with photographs of the **Arakan forest turtle**, an endangered creature that was thought to only live in the neighbouring country of Myanmar. The Mro people now work with conservationists as Tortoise Guardians to protect the species.

59

TREASURE IN NEW ZEALAND'S TUSSOCKS

Around 80 million years ago, a sliver of land broke away from the super landmass known as Gondwana, which includes Africa, Antarctica, Arabia, Australia, India, Madagascar and South America. It became the sunken continent of Zealandia, with just the rugged islands of New Zealand remaining above water the newly formed Tasman Sea. For many years it was isolated from the rest of the world and, in the absence of mammals or ground predators, unique birds evolved. This is especially true of the Fiordlands on the South Island, where mountains tower over mossy forests and mirror-like lakes.

A curious kea on a rocky slope, high above the snow, calls out as though 'laughing' – it's telling the other parrots that it wants to play. These intelligent birds toss rocks back and forth as if playing parrot tennis, or try to remove a rock from the other's mouths in a game of tug of war. It's all part of growing up as they learn to work together in large flocks.

Huge Haast's eagles once dominated the skies here. They were able to attack ostrich-like birds called moa that stood about 3.5 metres high. Although both of these species are now extinct, another prehistoric bird still calls the Fiordlands home . . .

60

The last thing you expect to find in a forest is a penguin. Yet these Tawaki (crested penguins) are perfectly at home within the trees, safely raising their fluffy chicks. Except something is missing here – fish to eat. When it's time to forage for food . . . *splash*! A forest stream makes an ideal shortcut to and from the sea.

A long, slender bill emerges from a burrow between the mossy roots of a tree. It's followed by the bowling-ball-like body of a Fiordland tokoeka (pronounced tok-oh-ay-kah), also known as a southern brown kiwi. Its hair-like feathers give it a shaggy appearance as it snuffles along the forest floor, using its bill to probe rotten logs or the ground in search of insects.

Since the Ice Ages, slow-moving rivers of ice have carved the landscape, creating high alpine lakes. And it was on the sandy shores of Lake Te Anau in 1948 that a hiker made a startling discovery: unfamiliar bird tracks, then an unusual call. Convinced it was the sound of an extinct bird, he traipsed through the tussocky grasses . . .

THE TAKAHĒ TAKES A STAND

There was a flash of red as two stout legs disappeared down an invisible trail. Eventually, a shiny, bauble-shaped bird stepped into the light; its blue-green feathers iridescent in the sun. After being missing for half a century, the prehistoric-looking takahē (pronounced ta-kaa-hay), a species of flightless bird, had been found. Its discovery revealed . . .

Takahēs were named by the indigenous Māori people to mean 'stand up tall and stamp your feet on the ground'.

Despite seventy years of conservation, the takahē remains one of the rarest bird species on the planet, with around 500 living in the wild.

Takahē eat the tussock grasses' starchy leaf base. The food's fibrous nature is responsible for each bird pooping enough to cover up to nine metres a day.

The Ngāi Tahu tribe are guardians of the takahē, which they value as *taonga*, or 'treasure'. They oversee the birds raised in captivity and ensure their remote habitat remains a protected wilderness.

63

FROM THE BACK OF BEYOND

AUSTRALIA'S COMEBACK CREATURES

Since European settlers first colonized Australia's sunburnt shores in 1788, more than 100 of its strange and unique species have vanished. And in recent times, Australia's extinction rate has become one of the highest on the planet, at nearly five species a decade. In the country's rain-starved Outback, hidden highlands and rugged islands, it would be all too easy for more species to disappear without anyone ever noticing they were gone. But thankfully Australians *are* taking notice, and in the country's wildest corners, they are finding Comeback Creatures still clinging on.

1. In 1918, a boat shipwrecked on wave-washed Lord Howe Island in the Tasman Sea released stowaway black rats onto the island's shores. Within a few years, the hungry rats had devoured the endemic **Lord Howe Island stick insect**, a creature with a hard shell that earned it the name 'tree lobster'. Then, one night in 2001, scientists climbed the world's tallest sea stack beyond the island's shore, and rediscovered a few of the stick insects clinging on to a tree . . . and life.

2. The **night parrot** was often referred to as a 'ghost bird' by indigenous tribes, because the nocturnal, ground-dwelling bird was so hard to spot in the spiky spinifex grasses. Not seen alive for a century, this rare bird was presumed extinct – and some wondered if it had ever really existed at all. Then, in 2013, after fifteen years and 17,000 hours searching, a keen wildlife detective took its photo. The area where the night parrot was found was turned into a reserve - its location secret to protect the species.

3. Named for its white back stripe and nail-like spur at the end of its tail, the **bridled nail-tail wallaby** was declared extinct in the 1930s. Around forty years later, in the small town of Dingo in Queensland's remote highlands, a man spotted wallabies with the same distinctive stripe while he was building a fence. A few years later, the government brought the property and turned it into a national park to protect the nail-tails.

65

LOST IN THE LAND OF DRAGONS ON FERNANDINA ISLAND

On remote Fernandina Island, part of the Galápagos Island chain in the Pacific Ocean, dragon-like iguanas swagger across the blackened earth. But instead of breathing fire, it boils beneath their feet. For although the iguanas appear to be rulers of this island, they have a dangerous neighbour: La Cumbre, one of the region's most active volcanoes. And every few years it explodes, sending red hot lava spilling down its slopes and into the sea. In this land of dragons, only the fearless survive.

Located about 1,000 kilometres from land, Fernandina Island's only animal inhabitants either flew, swam or drifted there on the waves many years ago, where they have evolved without competition from introduced species.

A pregnant land iguana hauls her hefty body up La Cumbre, one gruelling step at a time. She's on a mission to lay her eggs in the warm soil at the crater's edge, in a journey that can take ten days. But she's not the first to reach the top – other females have taken the best spots. Her only option is to make the treacherous journey into the volcano's rim to lay her eggs.

At the foot of the volcano, lava that once flowed has hardened to form jet-black lava fields. Although inhospitable for most life, the razor-sharp rocks and barren landscape is ideal for clusters of spiny lava cactus.

Tens of thousands of marine iguanas sunbathe on the jagged rocks along the shore, eyes closed as their salt encrusted bodies warm in the sun. Soon it's time to take the plunge, as one by one they leap into the sea. They're one of the world's only sea lizards able to dive down deep, to eat the algae that grows on the rocks below.

But not all animals thrive on this island. A giant once roamed its slopes, but disappeared over a century ago when its habitat was destroyed by one of La Cumbre's frequent eruptions. Then, fresh droppings and a glimpse of the giant from an aircraft inspired scientists in 2019 to set off on a mission to find it. And, at last, at the foot of the volcano . . .

67

FINDING FERNANDA

A Fernandina giant tortoise was found tucked inside a shrub, sheltering from the sun. Only one other Fernandina giant tortoise had ever been found – a male in 1906 that didn't survive. Compared to him, this female tortoise, nicknamed Fernanda, was much smaller; probably because the barren lava fields offered so few plants for her to eat.

Huge tracts of Fernandina Island remain unexplored because of the treacherous lava fields that cover much of the island.

The Galápagos Island chain earned its name from the old Spanish word *galapago*, which means 'saddle', because of the saddle-shaped shells of the resident tortoises.

Four species of giant tortoise were hunted to extinction. The remaining twelve species are all endangered, and all live on the Galápagos Islands.

Fernanda is now cared for in a tortoise sanctuary on a nearby island. In the meantime, scientists remain ever-hopeful of finding her a mate, after other tortoise tracks and scat were spotted on Fernandina Island. But is she the last of her kind?

THIS IS NOT THE END

It's more than possible that Fernanda the giant tortoise *is* the last of her kind. And when this happens, she will become known as an endling, as her species count will have sadly gone down . . . to one. When Fernanda dies, her species will likely die out, too. And so, all hope now rests with the scientists scouring her island home to find a male so that Fernanda can mate, and her species can be brought back from the brink of extinction.

But as hard as the scientists try, sometimes another mate cannot be found and the endlings live out their last days alone, often in captivity. In this way, we finally get to know their personalities and their plight . . .

Martha the **passenger pigeon** died in 1914 in the Cincinnati Zoo, USA. The rest of her species was over-hunted for food.

The last **thylacine** (a Tasmanian tiger) died in 1936 in Beaumaris Zoo, Australia. Its species was hunted to extinction.

Celia the **Pyrenean ibex** (a wild mountain goat) died in a Spanish national park in 2000. The others of her kind were hunted for sport.

Lonesome George, the **Pinta Island tortoise**, died in 2012 in a tortoise sanctuary on Santa Cruz Island. His species was hunted for food.

At the time of writing this book . . .

Only around 100 **Amur leopards** remain in the snowy wilds of Russia and China.
Perhaps only 50 **Javan rhinos** hide in an Indonesian national park.
In Mexico's Gulf of California, barely 10 **vaquitas** (a small porpoise) swim on.
Only two **northern white rhinos** remain . . . and both are female.

But we are not going to let any of them go without a fight.

MEANWHILE, IN A LABORATORY...

In a film called *Jurassic Park*, scientists discovered a way to bring dinosaurs back from the dead. Spoiler alert . . . it did *not* go to plan! While the idea of velociraptors racing alongside cars may seem far-fetched, it's not strictly the work of fiction. In fact, scientists are closer than you might think to creating new versions of extinct species using the science of de-extinction.

STRANGER THAN FICTION

To bring back the woolly mammoth, an animal that roamed the frozen tundra of the Arctic up until 4,000 years ago, scientists want to take DNA from its remains, such as from a tooth. The DNA would be inserted into an elephant egg that would then be implanted inside a female Asian elephant – the mammoth's closest living relative. The female could then give birth to a 'mammophant': a creature part woolly mammoth, part elephant, that could live on the Arctic's treeless tundra.

GREEN GRAZERS

And scientists are excited by the possibilities. Huge mammophants grazing the Arctic tundra would naturally knock down trees, allowing grasses to thrive. This could be a giant win in humanity's fight against global warming, as the grasses trap carbon dioxide gases that make the world hotter.

BUT IS IT THE RIGHT THING TO DO?

Imagine a world where dodos dawdle or Tasmanian tigers prowl, because scientists are working to bring those species back, too. However, in the thousands of years that certain animals have been gone, other species may have filled their space in the wild. If so, could bringing back extinct animals upset the balance in nature once more? Is pouring money and time into de-extinction a distraction from the threats facing living species?

What do you think? Should humans try to turn back time for those creatures we pushed to extinction in a rare chance to right a wrong? And what creatures would you like to see brought back from extinction, and why?

YOU CAN BE A WILDLIFE DETECTIVE!

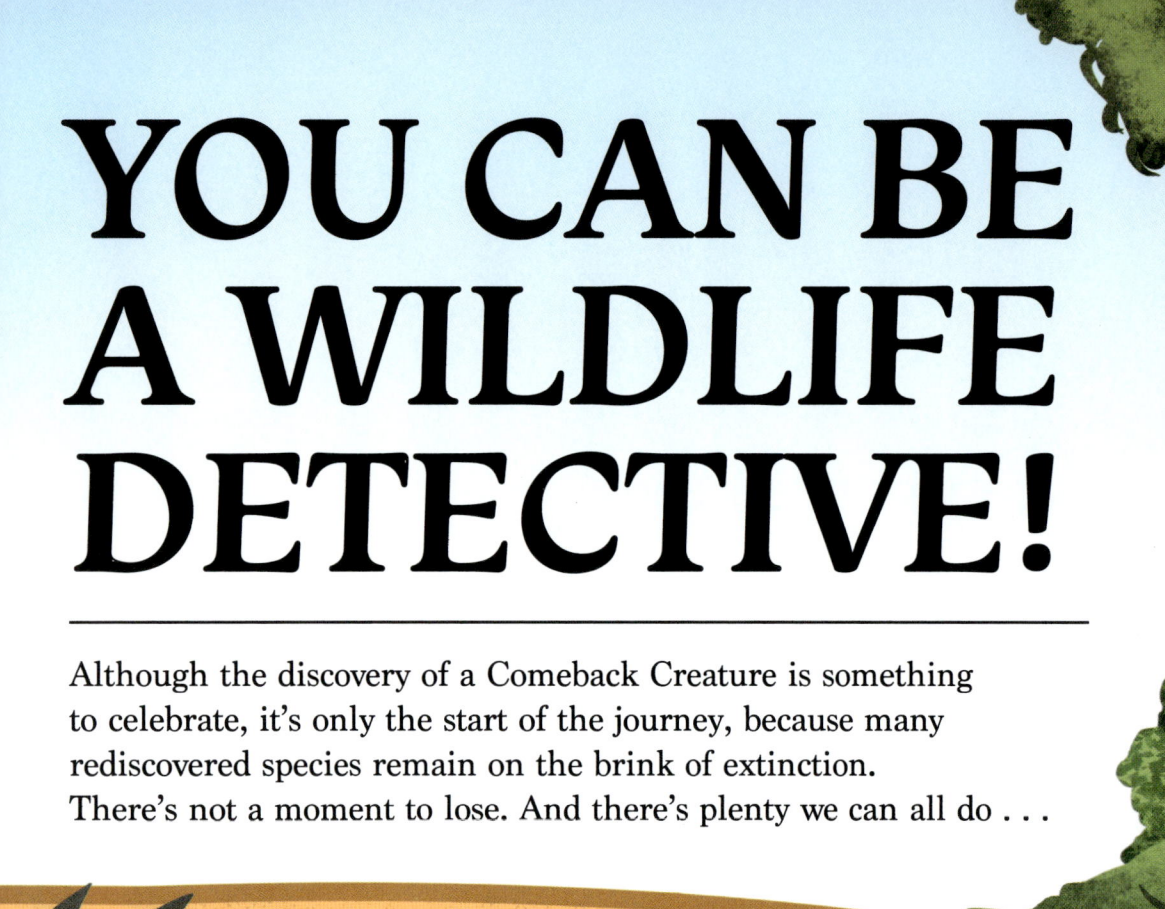

Although the discovery of a Comeback Creature is something to celebrate, it's only the start of the journey, because many rediscovered species remain on the brink of extinction. There's not a moment to lose. And there's plenty we can all do . . .

Take care of the special places where nature lives by joining in with clean-ups and tree plantings.

Learn about the endangered species in your area and give them a voice by telling everyone you know.

With an adult, volunteer your time to do research that will help scientists, from recording wildlife sightings to taking photos.

Discover more about animals and plants in danger of extinction by visiting the International Union for Conservation of Nature (IUCN) Red List. This database provides the extinction risk for 166,000 species – a number that grows every year. Find out where they are, how many there are, what's threatening their survival and what conservationists are doing to help protect them. Head to *iucnredlist.org* to get started.

Create spaces for animals to live in, from nest boxes and bug hotels to wildlife ponds and beehives.

Visit wildlife parks, zoos and reserves – you not only get a chance to enjoy nature, but your entrance fee supports work to conserve threatened species.

Always leave nature as you found it. Never take anything away other than the memories.

It's a big, wild world with lots of places to hide, which makes it hard to know when a species has truly disappeared. But with the help of science and people just like you, we have an opportunity to right what is wrong, and for nature to get an extraordinary second chance to make a comeback.

LONG LIVE THE COMEBACK CREATURES!

GLOSSARY

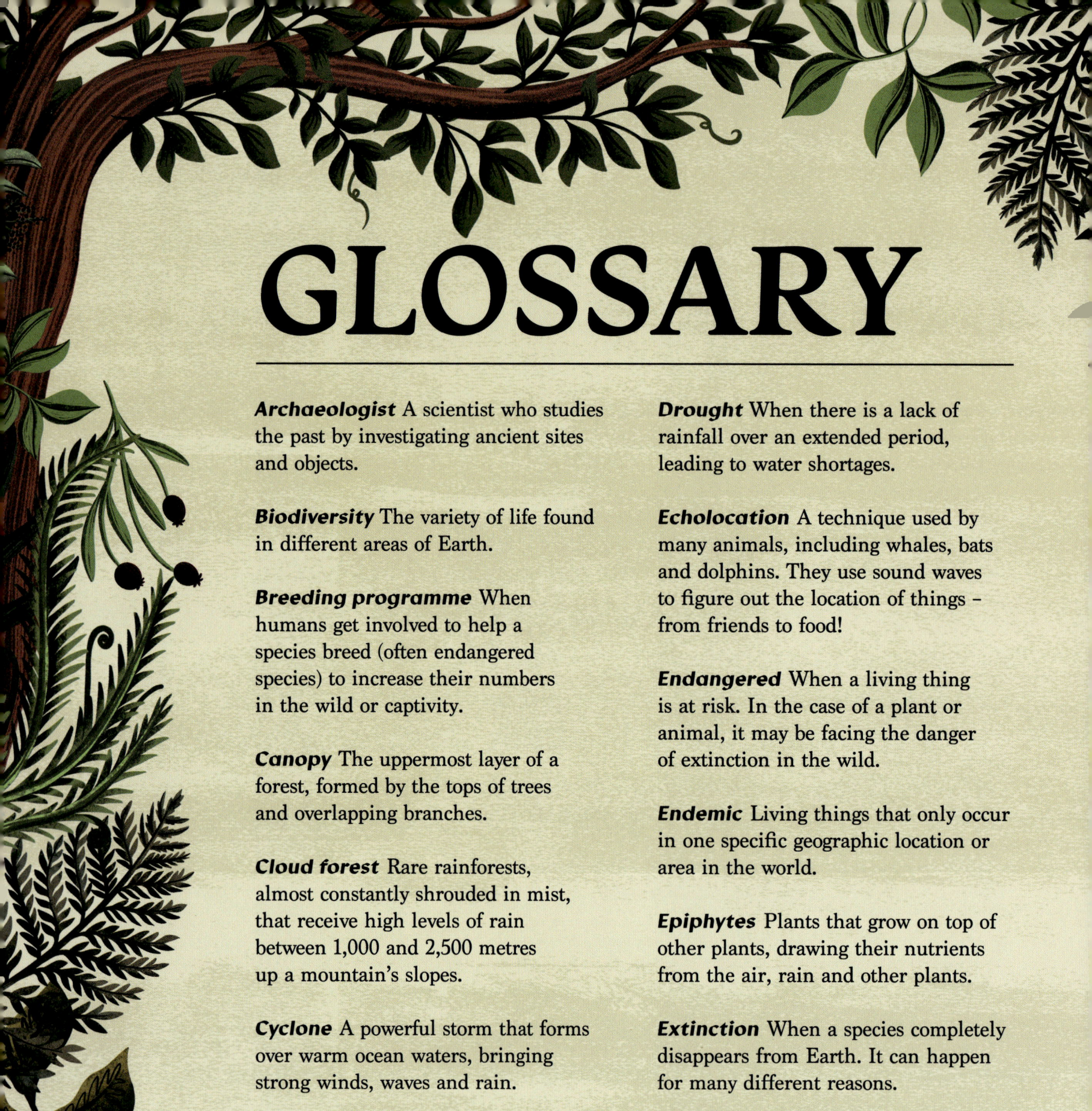

Archaeologist A scientist who studies the past by investigating ancient sites and objects.

Biodiversity The variety of life found in different areas of Earth.

Breeding programme When humans get involved to help a species breed (often endangered species) to increase their numbers in the wild or captivity.

Canopy The uppermost layer of a forest, formed by the tops of trees and overlapping branches.

Cloud forest Rare rainforests, almost constantly shrouded in mist, that receive high levels of rain between 1,000 and 2,500 metres up a mountain's slopes.

Cyclone A powerful storm that forms over warm ocean waters, bringing strong winds, waves and rain.

De-extinction Bringing a version of an extinct species back to life.

DNA A chemical found in the cells of living things that provides instructions for the body to grow and develop.

Drought When there is a lack of rainfall over an extended period, leading to water shortages.

Echolocation A technique used by many animals, including whales, bats and dolphins. They use sound waves to figure out the location of things – from friends to food!

Endangered When a living thing is at risk. In the case of a plant or animal, it may be facing the danger of extinction in the wild.

Endemic Living things that only occur in one specific geographic location or area in the world.

Epiphytes Plants that grow on top of other plants, drawing their nutrients from the air, rain and other plants.

Extinction When a species completely disappears from Earth. It can happen for many different reasons.

Fossils The preserved remains or impressions of plants and animals buried under layers of sand and mud, that eventually turn into rock.

Habitat A plant or animal's natural home, providing all the things it needs to survive – food, water and shelter.

Herpetologists Scientists who study reptiles and amphibians.

Hydroelectric dam A dam built across a river that turns energy created by water into electricity.

Ichthyologists Scientists who study fish.

Indigenous people People descended from a land's earliest human inhabitants.

Introduced species A species that isn't native to an area, but has been intentionally or accidentally brought there.

Lazarus taxon A living thing that reappears after being presumed extinct.

Magma Extremely hot liquid and semi-liquid rock, found beneath Earth's crust.

Mineral A solid substance that occurs naturally in the earth, for example crystals or gold.

Nocturnal Animals that are mainly active at night and sleep during the day.

Ornithologists Scientists who study birds.

Outback The sparsely populated part of Australia, far away from cities and towns, covering 81 per cent of the land.

Palaeontologists Scientists who study plant and animal fossils.

Peninsula A piece of land connected to the mainland on one side, but is otherwise surrounded by sea.

Plague A contagious disease, spread by rats, that was responsible for the death of millions of people throughout history.

Plankton A collection of tiny living things that float or drift in the sea or other water bodies

Plantation A large farm or estate where plants or trees are grown to make a profit.

Scat Animal droppings.

Sea stack A tall rocky column in the sea.

Taxon Living things organized into groups that share characteristics.

Tectonic plates The different solid rocky sections of Earth's crust, which fit together like a puzzle on the planet's surface.

The Bible A collection of ancient books and letters about the religion of Christianity.

Twilight Zone The cold, dark layer of the ocean, below its sunlit surface, reaching from 200 to 1,000 metres.

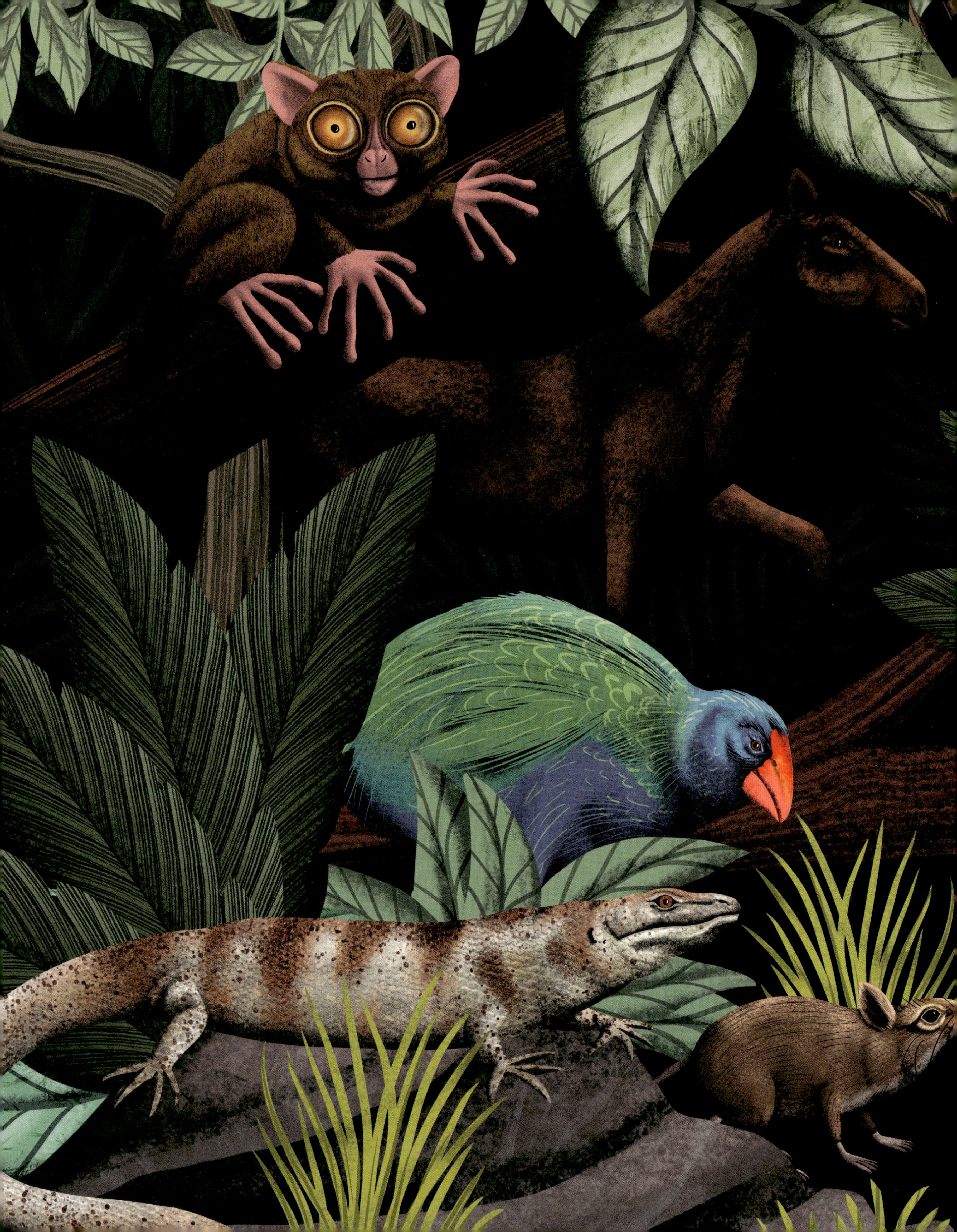

*For the Comeback Creatures.
Hang in there, guys!
L.S.S.*

*To Cat, for always being there.
L.R.*

Comeback Creatures © 2025 Quarto Publishing plc.
Text © 2025 Leisa Stewart-Sharpe. Illustrations © 2025 Lucy Rose.

First published in 2025 by Wide Eyed Editions,
an imprint of The Quarto Group.
1 Triptych Place, London, SE1 9SH, United Kingdom.
T (0)20 7700 6700 F (0)20 7700 8066 **www.Quarto.com**
EEA Representation, WTS Tax d.o.o., Žanova ulica 3, 4000 Kranj, Slovenia.

The right of Lucy Rose to be identified as the illustrator and Leisa Stewart-Sharpe to be identified as the author of this work has been asserted by them in accordance with the Copyright, Designs and Patents Act, 1988 (United Kingdom).

All rights reserved.

No part of this publication may be reproduced, stored in a retrieval system, or transmitted, in any form, or by any means, electrical, mechanical, photocopying, recording or otherwise without the prior written permission of the publisher or a licence permitting restricted copying.

A catalogue record for this book is available from the British Library.

ISBN 978-0-71128-835-5

The illustrations were created created in pencil and coloured digitally
Set in Marion, Monarcha, Manofa

Designers: Karissa Santos and Vanessa Lovegrove
Editors: Hannah Dove, Katie Taylor and Lucy Menzies
Production Controller: Robin Boothroyd
Commissioning Editor: Hannah Dove
Art Director: Karissa Santos
Publisher: Debbie Foy

Manufactured in Guangdong, China CC 092025

9 8 7 6 5 4 3 2 1